Virginia
on my mind

FALCON™

Design, typesetting, and other prepress work
by Falcon Press, Helena, Montana.
Printed in Korea.

Library of Congress Number: 90-55231

ISBN 1-56044-026-0

Front cover photos
THOMAS R. FLETCHER *Dogwood, Virginia's state flower and tree*
JOHN M. COFFMAN *Cardinal, Virginia's state bird*

Back cover photos
BILL TIERNAN *A welcoming at Norfolk Naval Base*
TOM ALGIRE *Governor's Palace at Williamsburg*
LARRY ULRICH *Dark Hollow Falls, Shenandoah National Park*

For extra copies of this book
Please check with your local bookstore, or write to
Falcon Press, P.O. Box 1718, Helena, MT 59624.
You also may call toll-free 1-800-582-BOOK.

Wild geraniums in Shenandoah National Park WILLARD CLAY

introduction

The Mona Lisa of America, Virginia teases us out of mind with a slight smile and air of gentle, dreamy repose. For years it had the reputation of being the most conservative of states, but behind that placid exterior swift changes have been occurring. In the 1960s it lifted barriers to voting and enlarged funds for human services. In 1970 its people ratified progressive changes when a half dozen other states were rejecting revisions of their constitutions. An influx of newcomers in the 1980s made Virginia in 1990 the sixth-fastest growing state, with nearly two-thirds of a population of six million residing in the urban crescent from northern Virginia to Hampton Roads.

Yet its people may draw upon a past in which Virginians led the struggle for independence and then supplied four of the first five presidents in framing the new government. They feel it has the capability of blending the best of the past with the demands of the future. And much of its heritage, natural and historic, abides.

The white tundra swan returns in September to the blue waters around Assateague Island off Virginia's Eastern Shore, setting back its giant wings like nylon chutes, thrusting out its black-webbed feet as buoys just before it touches down and settles on the water so softly not a feather is mussed, then furling its white wings as gracefully as a ballerina taking a bow.... Along Virginia Beach the whitecaps march, row on row, against the shore in the ceaseless war between surf and sand. Back of the beach in Seashore State Park, Spanish moss drapes the trees, greybeards, old soldiers reflecting over dark pools.... And in the midst of the million-strong metropolis of Hampton Roads, 375 black bears roam 106,000 acres of the Dismal Swamp Refuge spreading across portions of the cities of Chesapeake and Portsmouth and three North Carolina counties.

The storied James River, having journeyed from the mountains through the piedmont, tumbles across the rocks under Richmond's ramparts and winds in jumprope loops across the alluvial plain of Hampton Roads, reluctant to leave the land now, doubling on itself to look back where it has been, a Virginia river to the end.... The Blue Ridge Mountains, through a trick of the atmosphere, appear under the afternoon sun as a veil that might be parted with a hand. Between the Blue Ridge and the Alleghenies runs the Great Valley along which pioneers moved westward. In the fall, Virginians make a pilgrimage there, marveling at the mountainsides aflame with foliage of red, orange, bronze, and yellow as if thronged with jostling Indians in war paint and feathers descending to reclaim their lands, while ahead of them scrub pines crouch on the Valley floor, reconnoitering scouts, amid the broom straw....

Virginia's mountains, worn down by time, are a grandfatherly lot. The Skyline Drive wriggles 105 miles along the top of the Blue Ridge Parkway through 194,000 acres of Shenandoah National Park, which claims sixty peaks between three thousand and four thousand feet high. Near Bedford are the Peaks of Otter, Flat Top, and Sharp Top. With a coxcomb crest of boulders, Sharp Top seems a rostrum from which to address the universe. John Randolph of Roanoke was so moved by the view he commanded his servant to join him in prayer. At Afton, Skyline Drive changes to Blue Ridge Parkway and continues 217 miles into North Carolina. Once a sea lapped at the Blue Ridge's western slopes. When the hills hump their backs through morning mists, the waters seem to have come · again, with whales.

In southwest Virginia is Mount Rogers, a vast mountain tableland once crowned with prime spruce and fir. At the century's turn, lumber companies began building railroads into the high country, bought timber rights from the mountaineers for a new shotgun, cut thousands of acres, then set fire to the slash and debris. The flames, seen for miles writhing on the mountain, cracked rock pinnacles. The plateau in the sky came back in grassland. Lavender mountain laurel and purple rhododendron run riot amid gray house-sized boulders in the spring. The air is hushed and clean, and it is worth a trip just to breathe it.

It was here, on the slopes of Mount Rogers, I visited Catherine Blevins, berry picking near her cabin above a creek. Catherine churned butter and sent it to town at fifty cents a pound, which brought $68 to feed the cow and the hog, she said, as if that was as much as anybody had a right to expect, a balancing of the books with nature. Her eyes were as blue as the sky reflected in the mountain spring, and as untroubled; her face, untouched by cosmetics, was ruddy as a fall apple, lovely under a crown of white hair pulled back into a knot and streaked yellow with the sun.

Catherine visited her seven children (and twenty-four great-grandchildren), but insisted on staying with the cabin. From her garden she gathered and canned vegetables and fruits. In the morning, she built a fire in the wood cookstove and went to turn in the cow with the calf and fed the pig and came back to get her breakfast and went back and milked the cow after the calf got through. So she went until night fell on the mountain, a slow, soft blanket. She was at one

A ruby-throated hummingbird enjoying nectar from a Mexican sunflower JOHN M. COFFMAN

A fisherman's sunrise at Virginia Beach   RAYMOND GEHMAN

with the seasons, as deliberate and steady as their turning. The sweetness and integrity of her life is replicated by the watermen on the coast.

Such as Tom Reed, a "munger," (one who makes a living from the marsh and the sea), who became a valued assistant with federal wildlife research teams. His face is as tan and unlined as hard-packed sand. He is as sturdy as the wild ponies that are rounded up each July for sale to support the volunteer fire department in Chincoteague. He fits Jefferson's vision of a man at one with nature and work. His voice is the sort a person would expect to hear when putting a seashell to the ear, with a forthright sounding of the vowel "o" so that the pronoun "I" becomes full-bodied "Oy" and time becomes "toime." To dig clams, he wore a blue flannel shirt, oilskin coat, and linen moccasins. "You'd curl your foot around a clam, with a dab of mud and then—quick!—with the pressure of the water and the mud, you'd rake it up. 'Leggin' 'em,' we called it. When the water's deeper, you hold the clam between your feet, bear your weight on the boat, and you jump and catch 'em. It was hard. A lot of toimes I dreaded to go in the cold, but it was a rewarding loif, it seems to me loike, and I believe if I had to live my loif over again, I'd loike to do the same thing."

Virginia cityscapes excite, too. Set amid Richmond's skyscrapers is Capital Square, a green hill topped by the columned, oyster-gray Statehouse designed by

Thomas Jefferson. Centered in the Rotunda between the House and Senate of the General Assembly is a statue beyond compare, the life-size marble likeness of George Washington, done from life by Jean Houdon. Wearing his old military coat from which two buttons were missing, Washington was 53, done with war but not yet elected to the presidency. Houdon worked two weeks trying to get just the right expression on Washington's face. Along came a mule trader to Mount Vernon and when the trader mentioned a price, Washington's mouth tightened—and Houdon had him. Between the two chambers, legislators pause to trade beneath Father Washington's severe and steady stare.

In Hampton Roads, on the horizons of Norfolk, Portsmouth, and Newport News, loom sixteen-story, orange-limbed Martian monsters: double-hoist cranes that keep Virginia ports competitive as the fastest-growing, fastest-working piers on the East Coast. Newport News ports connect with CSX trains and Norfolk's piers tie in with the Norfolk Southern Railway. In Roanoke are the world's finest railroad shops. Occasionally, they fire up one of the old mighty steam locomotives for an excursion. When the locomotive whistles, the steam gives its voice a hoarse, haunting, living quality, and people in Big Lick lift their heads and smile at the sound.

Anchoring Hampton Roads' sprawling military complex is the Norfolk Naval Base, offering the moving spectacle of families waiting on the pier to welcome five thousand men standing at attention around the flight deck of a huge carrier, the ship nosing around the river's bend and slowly halting like an immense mesa beside the multitude. You can feel the tides of passion as those on deck and dock strain to pick loved ones out of the masses. Then the sailors come pounding like rapids down the gangplanks until, in a whirlpool of emotions, families are whole again waltzing in each other's arms, pounding backs, crying, laughing. The pier empties gradually as they leave arm-in-arm, children riding their father's shoulders, receding to homes across the country while the great ship sits quietly, waiting.

Despite television's leveling effect, Virginians' accents persist. Let a Virginian listen, blindfolded, to talk anywhere in the state and he or she can identify the place. If a visiting Englishman encountered the broad "a," still passed around like a cup of tea (or glass of sherry) among members of some of the old families of Richmond and upper Tidewater, he might conclude he was on the Thames instead of the James. In the classic accent prevalent in Richmond, plain "house" becomes "how-oos." Ordinary "out" becomes "ow-oot" and "about" is transformed into "abaa-oot." You will recognize them when you hear them, as I did once during a high school performance of "Macbeth." When Lady Macbeth strayed on stage, sleep-walking, washing her hands, she intoned: "Ow-oo-ut, ow-oo-ut, da-yum spah-woot!"—as if she were turning a naughty dog into the night. Occasionally, still, you hear a Virginian insert a "y" into a word, so that "garden" becomes "gahden" and "car" is "cyah." It makes life seem ever so much finer, somehow.

In southwest Virginia, a teacher told her pupils the Christmas story about the three wise men arriving from afar to offer gifts to the babe in the manger. She asked her fourth-graders to come dressed next day in Christmas costumes. One boy, whose father was a volunteer fireman, came wearing a magnificent red fireman's helmet. But what, the teacher asked the child, did a fireman's hat have to do with the Christmas story?

"Didn't you tell us that the three wise men come from a far?" the boy replied.

The Old Dominion's reputation for hospitality traces to colonial times when Virginians thirsted for word from the outside world. They would seize a stranger and hold him or her enthralled for days like Circe charmed and penned the sailors of Odysseus. All a traveler had to do was inquire upon the road where any gentleman lived, and he could count on being welcomed. Visitors left accounts as if Virginians were a fabulous race of the sort Gulliver found. "Almost every person keeps a horse," marveled one, "and I have known some spending the morning ranging several miles in the woods to find and catch their horses to ride two or three miles to Church, to the Court House, or to a Horse Race."

Visiting still is a prime amusement, evident in the reluctance of two Virginia women to part after a long talk. They will be on the verge, at last, of saying goodbye, their husbands stirring into life by the cars on which they have been leaning, when suddenly one woman, in the act of putting her foot in the car to depart, will say, "Oh, by the way, I heard the other day from Betsy Lou!" Off they go on another round of conversation. The men lapse again against the cars.

Festivals flourish in Virginia from April to October. These convivial gatherings feature oysters, country ham (long cure and short), barbecued beef, pork, and chicken, baked shad, maple syrup, apple butter, shrimp, crabs, peaches, peanuts.... One could live nine months a year simply by attending each day's groaning board.

Nearly every step one takes here is on hallowed ground. Two-thirds of the battles of the Civil War—that dark "Hamlet" of the American soul, Bruce Catton called it—were fought in Virginia. To grasp the

tragedy, view any battlefield. At Cold Harbor on June 3, 1864, General Grant threw sixty thousand troops, half his army, against Lee's entrenched men. The night before, the Federal soldiers had heard the Confederates digging in. Grant's men knew they would face death and many pinned their names and addresses to their coats before they went into battle. The assault lasted eight minutes—and eight thousand Union soldiers fell.

Go, for the nation's beginning, to Jamestown. There in 1607, 105 settlers disembarked from three tiny ships to undertake the first English settlement in the New World, nineteen years before the Pilgrims touched Plymouth Rock. Now and then a tourist marches into the Jamestown museum and asks, "Where is the rock?" The colony survived thanks to a stocky soldier, Captain John Smith, and an Indian teenager, Pocahontas, daughter of Emperor Powhatan. "He that will not worke will not eat," Smith declared, and he would pour a dipper of cold water down a layabout's sleeve. Pocahontas slipped through the woods to warn the settlers of impending Indian raids. That child of a Stone Age civilization visited and charmed the Court of St. James' in London. As she lay dying, her last words were to her sorrowing husband, settler John Rolfe, about their son. "What does it matter so long as the child liveth?" she asked. He thrived, as did the colony she had saved. "The mother of us all," poet Vachel Lindsay called her.

After fires and malaria beset Jamestown, the settlers moved to higher ground at Williamsburg, which became the training ground for statesmen. There Thomas Jefferson whetted his intellect. Patrick Henry cried treason against the British crown. George Washington put on his uniform for the French and Indian Wars and honed the skills he turned against the British in the American Revolution. John Marshall learned law from George Wythe. A few miles away at Yorktown, on a bluff overlooking the York River, lies the battlefield where Washington, with the aid of the French, trapped General Cornwallis and his Redcoats in 1781 and won American independence. In the visitors center is his headquarter's tent. For eight years Americans' hopes for freedom were pinned on that patch of canvas. Didn't make any difference how many battles the Americans lost, a French observer reported to his king. In the end they would win the war because they had Washington. At the Battle of Monmouth, his troops in a rout, Washington appeared on his white charger, as if dropped from the sky, to rally them. A major covered his eyes, fearful he might see Washington fall in the hail of bullets. The war ended, all Washington wanted was to farm Mount Vernon. The American people had other ideas.

Near Mount Vernon on the Potomac River is Gunston Hall, the elegant little mansion of

Yellow buds of an early-blooming crocus breaking through a lingering snowbank WILLIAM B. FOLSOM

George Mason, who was always reluctant to leave it. Inside is the table on which he wrote Virginia's Declaration of Rights, which became the basis of the nation's Bill of Rights. Mason, a leader in framing the U.S. Constitution, refused to sign it when the convention recognized slavery and failed to include a Bill of Rights. James Madison, who lived at Montpelier, near Jefferson's Monticello, saw that the first amendments to the Constitution included the Bill of Rights. In Richmond is the home of John Marshall, the fourth and great Chief Justice who made the U.S. Supreme Court supreme with his finding that the Court had the power to review the constitutionality of the acts of Congress. "I went in the army a Virginian, and I came out an American," Marshall said. He died in Philadelphia. As his body was borne to the ship that would take it home, the Liberty Bell tolled, and it was then that it cracked.

Stratford Hall in Westmoreland County was the home of the five Lee brothers who served their country during the Revolution. Both Richard Henry Lee and Francis Lightfoot Lee signed the Declaration of Independence. A sixth brother, a Tory, sat out the war on the sidelines. The Lees formed an axis with John Adams of Massachusetts who called them, "A band of brothers, intrepid and unchangeable..." who stood in the gap like the Greeks at Thermopylae.

As Washington led the fighting, Thomas Jefferson did the writing of newly won rights into the Virginia law. "Our Revolution," he wrote later, "presented us with an album on which we could write what we pleased." Jefferson would be astonished at the splendid condition of Monticello, his home near Charlottesville. As with many patriots who pledged their lives, fortunes, and sacred honor to achieve freedom, Jefferson died broke. But the cannonball clock is still rigged over Monticello's entrance. His other labor-saving devices—dumbwaiter, revolving bookcase, duplicator of correspondence—are in readiness. He'd be elated that the University of

Virginia, which he founded as the "bantling" of his old age, is flourishing. In a 1976 poll of American architects, a majority choose as the nation's "proudest achievement" in architecture the University's green lawn between the two long rows of two-story pavilions headed by the towering Rotunda. The vast sunlit expanse under the Rotunda's domed skylight is often termed America's most beautiful room.

Jefferson failed in efforts to abolish slavery, but he was able to exclude it from the Northwest Territory. He and the other founders left tools with which to continue their works. In Virginia two strands contend in creative tension. One hearkens to the past, clinging to what we know and cherish. The other, receiving a powerful thrust from Jefferson, looks to the future and things as they might better be. "I steer my bark with Hope in the head, leaving fears astern," Jefferson wrote John Adams.

Declining to join the citizens in Washington, D.C., in celebrating the fiftieth anniversary of the Declaration of Independence, Jefferson wrote on June 24, 1826: "All our eyes are opened, or opening, to the right of man. The general spread of the light of science has already laid open to every view the palpable truth, that the mass of mankind has not been born with saddles on their backs, nor a favored few booted and spurred, ready to ride them legitimately, by the grace by God. There are grounds of Hope for others. For ourselves let the annual return of this day forever refresh our recollections of these rights, and an undiminished devotion to them...."

On that Fourth of July both Jefferson and Adams died. Not knowing that his Virginia friend had preceded him in death by a little time, Adams said in his dying words: "Thomas Jefferson lives."

As do all the great patriots.

Guy Friddell
Norfolk

A whitetail doe standing backlit by the golden haze of sunrise, Albemarle County   JAMES FRANK

Moonrise over Hawksbill Mountain, Shenandoah National Park   CUB KAHN

   " *There is a name. Virginia. . . . It sings itself. . . . In the sweet, undulating roll of Virginia, you catch the soft folds of the Blue Ridge Mountains in the morning mist, the giddy, gaudy green Easter Egg hills billowing around Albemarle, the lazy James embracing Richmond, the dark green tobacco fields somnolent in the Southside sun, and the long, pale green combers rolling in white thunder on Virginia beach. . . .* **"**

Guy Friddell,
What Is It About Virginia?

Fog-shrouded symbols of Virginia—a tall oak and wild azalea in the Blue Ridge Mountains WILLARD CLAY

Maple seeds   JOHN M. COFFMAN

Red-leaved sweetgum and green-needled loblolly pine competing for attention in Seashore State Park, near Virginia Beach   CARR CLIFTON

66 Sometimes a slight haze, like a velvet mantle, veils the distant peaks. Sometimes a storm breaks over the mountains, thunder rattles among the crags, and all is hidden by rain. Then as the clouds lift, the mountains emerge dimly from the mist, like giants struggling to be free. 99

Virginius Dabney,
Virginius Dabney's Virginia

"Like giants struggling to be free"—the Blue Ridge Mountains from McAfee's Knob near Roanoke   FRED CRAMER

12

A dense patch of yellow lady's slippers, some of Virginia's loveliest wild orchids   WILLARD CLAY

Male Baltimore oriole above its deep, pendant nest   JOHN M. COFFMAN

Gray tree frog, a seldom seen but frequently heard resident of Virginia's moist woodlands   STEVEN Q. CROY

Matched pair of Canada geese investigating a coastal pond   LYNDA RICHARDSON

" If today one should wonder how that Tidewater countryside appeared to Washington's eyes, the answer is: much as it does now. For to a degree largely unmatched in America, the region resembles in topography its ancient, earliest configuration. "

William Styron,
The Quiet Dust

Seaside of Virginia's eastern shore near Hog Island Bay   JOHN M. HALL

Red-winged blackbird in silhouette, Chincoteague National Wildlife Refuge CUB KAHN

Dawn of a new day over Stony Man Mountain, Shenandoah National Park   CUB KAHN

Common egrets at rest and play in Chincoteague National Wildlife Refuge, Assateague Island   GLENN VAN NIMWEGEN

❝ ...Assateague belonged to the wild things—to the wild birds that nested on it, and the wild ponies whose ancestors had lived on it since the days of the Spanish galleon. ❞

Marguerite Henry,
Misty of Chincoteague

Wetlands along the northern end of Assateague Island   ROBERT PERRON

Pony roll on Assateague Island   D. L. WINSTON

A wild filly steps out on Assateague   D. L. WINSTON

Handsome descendant of Spanish mustangs, Assateague Island   ZIG LESZCZYNSKI / ANIMALS ANIMALS

Sunset over an abandoned oyster watcher's house, Tom's Cove, Assateague Island   GLENN VAN NIMWEGEN

Dawn along the shore of Virginia Beach   CATHERINE KARNOW

❝ *This is a noble sea. Calm and hospitable, majestic in size.
Its potential cannot be imagined.* **❞**

Captain John Smith

Red sky in morning, sailors take warning   MAE SCANLAN

Virginia Beach   CATHERINE KARNOW

Summer fun on Buckroe Beach in Hampton   CATHERINE KARNOW

You can never have too much suntan lotion   CATHERINE KARNOW

In training on Grandview Beach CATHERINE KARNOW

Enjoying the view at Virginia Beach CATHERINE KARNOW

Skateboarders properly attired at Virginia Beach   CATHERINE KARNOW

"I'd give up my other tooth for a bite."   CATHERINE KARNOW

Rolling in from the frothy Atlantic   MAE SCANLAN

❝ *Chaos! The surf seems to bellow as it explodes rhythmically against the beach here. And the beach whispers back, ever so improbably—order.* **❞**

Tom Horton,
Bay Country

Atlantic loggerhead hatchlings heeding the call of the sea, Back Bay National Wildlife Refuge   LYNDA RICHARDSON

Peaceful scene on Norfolk Pier CATHERINE KARNOW

66 *There is such a thing as honor. Virginians have lived for it, died for it . . .* 99

Virginia Moore,
Virginia Is a State of Mind

Portsmouth (foreground) and Norfolk, near the mouth of Hampton Roads   CATHERINE KARNOW

Richmond skyline from across the James River   CATHERINE KARNOW

The State Capitol, serving Virginia since 1788   CATHERINE KARNOW

Virginia state seal on a doorknob in the Capitol   JAMES FRANK

Family outing at Maymont Park in Richmond   CATHERINE KARNOW

Future artists at the Museum of Fine Arts in Richmond   CATHERINE KARNOW

Azaleas in full bloom   MAE SCANLAN

Oak-guarded Westover Plantation, built in 1734 and still resplendent, east of Richmond   DEREK FELL

The Shirley Plantation, built in 1724, one of the earliest
tobacco plantations in the New World   CATHERINE KARNOW

The Berkeley Plantation, ancestral home of two presidents—
William Henry Harrison and his grandson, Benjamin Harrison   CATHERINE KARNOW

Green tree frog in full voice on a pickerelweed leaf   FREDERICK D. ATWOOD

" *Outside, the night was filled with sound. The high mechanical screech of the cicadas was a metallic din which gradually whined into silence. A turtle dove called. His mate answered, far off, and then her voice sounded again and his voice cried out, closer now. In the distance, flowing over the pine trees, from the swamp, over the pond, came the thousand-voice choir of frogs. Once only came the saddest sound in the world, the single unanswered voice of a whippoorwill. . . .* **"**

Earl Hamner, Jr.,
Spencer's Mountain

Freshwater marsh from the Colonial Parkway, along the James River   DAVID MUENCH

> **The beauty of the Blue Ridge is a soft, feminine beauty, whereas that of the Alps, the Andes, or the Rockies, with their glaciers and avalanches, is awe-inspiring and terrible.** "

Virginius Dabney,
Virginius Dabney's Virginia

Late afternoon over the Massanutten and Allegheny mountains   CUB KAHN

Shenandoah Valley farm   JEFF GNASS

" To define the Shenandoah is an impossible and an unnecessary task. It is better merely to admire it, and to select here and there a dimple or a contour that catches our fancy. "

Wallace Nutting,
Virginia Beautiful

Colors of fall across the Shenandoah Valley CARR CLIFTON

Virginia's state flower and tree, the dogwood   WILLARD CLAY

" *Mountains are giant, restful, absorbent. You can heave your spirit into a mountain and the mountain will keep it, folded, and not throw it back as some creeks will. The creeks are the world with all its stimulus and beauty; I live there. But the mountains are home.* "

Annie Dillard,
Pilgrim at Tinker Creek

Falls on Cedar Run, Shenandoah National Park   WILLARD CLAY

White Oak Run cascading through White Oak Canyon, Shenandoah National Park   WILLARD CLAY

Unknown soldier's grave,
Arlington National Cemetery   MAE SCANLAN

Members of the Old Guard, past and present
WILLIAM B. FOLSOM / ARMY MAGAZINE

" *No other cemetery can compare to Arlington. The list of persons buried there is an index to the Nation's history* "

Guy Friddell,
The Virginia Way

Iwo Jima Memorial in Arlington   CATHERINE KARNOW

A peaceful scene along Wilderness Run,
where Confederate and Union troops fought in May 1864   DAVID MUENCH

*❝ The deeds that shook a continent belong to history. Farewell;
sound taps! And then a generation new must face its battles in its
turn, forever heartened by that heritage. ❞*

Douglas Southall Freeman,
Virginia Reader: A Treasury of Writings

A Confederate surgeon's amputating kit   WILLIAM B. FOLSOM

Confederate corporal   WILLIAM B. FOLSOM

Cedar Mountain Confederates re-enacting the Battle of Cedar Mountain   WILLIAM B. FOLSOM

The *Susan Constant, Discovery,* and *Godspeed,* replicas of settlers' ships, docked at Jamestown Festival Park   TOM ALGIRE

❝ *. . . the Countrie (for the moste part) on each side plaine high ground, with many fresh Springes, the people in all places kindely intreating us, daunsing and feasting us with strawberries Mulberies, Bread, Fish, and other their Countrie provisions wherof we had plenty. . .* **❞**

Captain John Smith,
1607

Passmore Creek on Jamestown Island   MAE SCANLAN

Church tower at Jamestown, erected in 1639 and the oldest brick structure in the United States   MAE SCANLAN

A settler's view of sunset over the James River, Jamestown National Historic Site   MAE SCANLAN

Grocer's sign, Williamsburg   STEVE SOLUM

The Governor's Palace, built between 1708 and 1720, in Williamsburg   MAE SCANLAN

Preparing a colonial meal at the Governor's Palace   JOHN LEWIS STAGE / THE IMAGE BANK

Muskets and bayonets, functional wall decorations at the Governor's Palace   JAMES FRANK

The Magazine, built in 1715 to house guns, ammunition, and gunpowder at Williamsburg   DAVID MUENCH

" *The more I have ranged the country the more I admire it. I have seen the best countries in Europe; I protest unto you, before the living God, put them all together, (and) this country will be equivalent unto them if it be inhabit(ed) with good people.* "

Sir Thomas Dale,
1613

Cheers at Chowning's, Williamsburg   CATHERINE KARNOW

Cobblers at work   JOHN LEWIS STAGE / THE IMAGE BANK

Fine millinery and fine flute music, Williamsburg
CATHERINE KARNOW

A wide-angle view of Alexandria City Hall, built in 1817 and rebuilt after a fire in 1871   CATHERINE KARNOW

Toy shop in Alexandria   CATHERINE KARNOW

Gardens at Virginia House, a 12th-century monastery shipped from England
and reassembled in Virginia in the 1920s by U.S. Ambassador Alexander Weddell   GENE AHRENS

Interior of Virginia House   CATHERINE KARNOW

The old mulberry tree at the Moore House, Yorktown   DAVID MUENCH

The surrender room in the Moore House, where Lord Cornwallis surrendered to General Washington in 1781   CONNIE TOOPS

Dressing up in colonial attire   GARY CRALLE / THE IMAGE BANK

Monticello, Thomas Jefferson's beloved home   DAVID MUENCH

" *I am as happy nowhere else and in no other society, and all my wishes end, where I hope my days will end, at Monticello.* "

Thomas Jefferson,
1789

Bust of Jefferson at the University of Virginia   MAE SCANLAN

A portion of the grounds at Mount Vernon   MAE SCANLAN

Cupola atop Mount Vernon   CATHERINE KARNOW

Mount Vernon   MAE SCANLAN

❝ *I can truly say I had rather be at Mount Vernon with a friend or two about me, than to be attended at the seat of government by the officers of state and the representatives of every power in Europe.* **❞**

George Washington,
letter written in 1790

Easter bonnets and belles in Richmond   TIM WRIGHT

  ❝ *Virginians are the most unmitigated, incorrigible, thoroughgoing, unqualified, consummate, whole-hog, glaring, flagrant, enormous, fabulous, perfect, stark, radical, downright, pure, headlong, rampant, irregardless, tooth-and-nail, devil-may-care, bull-at-the-gate individualists in the world. If you do not know this, you will never know Virginians. It is the key to their character. And this, I claim, is a phenomenon at a time when 'the individual withers and the world is more and more.'* ❞

Virginia Moore,
Virginia Is a State of Mind

Shiny trophies and antique automobiles at Rohr's Antiques in Manassas   CATHERINE KARNOW

Aboard the *Caper* at Norfolk   CATHERINE KARNOW

A day's catch, Norfolk   CATHERINE KARNOW

A local bicycle race in McLean   WILLIAM B. FOLSOM

A rip-roaring ride at Kings Dominion near Doswell   TIM WRIGHT

Off and running at the Richmond Newspapers Marathon   P. A. GORMAS

Great blue heron matching the color of the morning, Assateague Island   GLENN VAN NIMWEGEN

" *...Virginia is the land of the golden mean. The winter begins late and the spring comes early, and there is a gentleness, an unsentimental sweetness in the air...* **"**

Virginia Moore,
Virginia Is a State of Mind

Birdfoot violet brightening a Virginia wood CONNIE TOOPS

Redbuds decorating the banks of the Shenandoah River   SCOTT T. SMITH

" April and May are the liveliest time of year, when the trees and shrubs of Virginia are in bloom—the soft white and pink dogwood, redbud, wild azalea, crab apple and forsythia. "

Michael Frome,
Virginia

Opossums look odd anywhere, even in redbud trees   ERWIN & PEGGY BAUER

Dogwood blossoms   CUB KAHN

Whitetail fawn   JOHN M. COFFMAN

Cardinal flower   JOHN M. COFFMAN

" Spring was running in a thin green flame over the Valley. There was a mist of green on the trees; luminous patches of green and blue sprinkled the earth. The deeper hollows were thatched with shade, and all the little hills, just touched by sunlight, were carved into stillness. "

Ellen Glasgow,
Vein of Iron

Foggy morning in the Blue Ridge Mountains   WILLARD CLAY

Newly hatched box turtle discovering the world   FREDERICK D. ATWOOD

Praying mantis, waiting for the unwary   FREDERICK D. ATWOOD

Fishing, Virginia style CATHERINE KARNOW

Alluring colors CATHERINE KARNOW

Bald eagle along Virginia's northern coast   FRANK OBERLE / PHOTOGRAPHIC RESOURCES

Bobwhite quail on the lookout   LYNDA RICHARDSON

Mountain laurel   WILLARD CLAY

" *The autumn wind, like racing sunlight, had shaken down a rain of leaves. In the slanting shower she could see the crimson pink of the dogwood, the purplish velvet of the oaks, the clear gold of the hickories and beeches, the wavering flame of the maples, the fugitive scarlet of the black gum, and the tarnished bronze of the sycamores, walnuts, and poplars—all driven by streamers of mist toward the dark background of the pines. The air sparkled like new cider, the pines droned in the wind, the sun blazed on the splendor.* "

Ellen Glasgow,
Vein of Iron

Terrapin Mountain cloaked in fall colors,
Jefferson National Forest near Peaks of Otter   CARR CLIFTON

Autumn mushrooms, Jamestown Island   JEFF GNASS

Chipmunk stuffing itself for the winter   JOHN M. COFFMAN

Red-shouldered hawk, keen-eyed resident of Virginia's woodlands FREDRICK D. ATWOOD

Dogwood leaves heralding autumn   DAVID MUENCH

" *Then autumn comes, with all its pageantry, and the mountains and the valleys flame with gold and scarlet. As far as the eye can reach, a carpet of color stretches to the horizon.* "

Virginius Dabney,
Virginius Dabney's Virginia

Spicebush swallowtail caterpillar showing the large eye-like markings that confuse and discourage predators   JOHN M. COFFMAN

Flags of fall, sassafras leaves in
George Washington National Forest   CUB KAHN

Whitetail buck   ALAN D. BRIERE

" *What he saw was fixed forever in his mind, the dull gray sky of the winter morning, the barren limbs of the sleeping trees, the virgin snow and the great deer which stood silent, immobile, and enduring through all of memory.* **"**

Earl Hamner Jr.,
Spencer's Mountain

Maple leaves and winter's first snow   JOHN M. COFFMAN

A cardinal, Virginia's state bird, surveying a snowfall   JOHN M. COFFMAN

Frosted leaves   FRANK OBERLE / PHOTOGRAPHIC RESOURCES

" The sun was going down in a blaze, but as it sank behind the hills it shot up again in a fountain of light and scattered a sparkling spray into the clouds. "

Ellen Glasgow,
Vein of Iron

Sunset on oyster beds, Chincoteague   ROBERT C. SIMPSON

Water tupelo trees in the Dismal Swamp   ROBERT E. LYONS

“ *The Great Dismal Swamp! The legendary land of untamed wild beauty astride the Virginia and North Carolina border—where dense forests sprout from spongy peat ground, threaded by canals and ditches, many grown over like green tunnels untouched by sunlight.* ”

Michael Frome,
Virginia

Gray squirrel   CUB KAHN

Bobcat out on a limb   TIM CHRISTIE

The fine art of whittling at the Museum of
Frontier Culture in Staunton   WILLIAM B. FOLSOM

A frontier feast, Museum of Frontier Culture
WILLIAM B. FOLSOM

*" Time moved as slowly through the seasons as a great mill
grinding the grain of conversation, sifting it fine, polishing it and
the stories. It still does in many places in Virginia. "*

Guy Friddell,
The Virginia Way

Airborne over Fauquier County CATHERINE KARNOW

Girl Scouts, merry and meritorious   CATHERINE KARNOW

"The great human law that in the end recognizes and rewards merit is everlasting and universal."

Booker T. Washington

Humble beginnings, the birthplace cabin of Booker T. Washington, near Hardy DAVID MUENCH

Tobacco road   STEVE SOLUM

Saving the season's best, Warrenton Farmers Market   CATHERINE KARNOW

Fresh from the fields   CATHERINE KARNOW

Summiting on Mount Rogers, at 5,729 feet Virginia's highest point   FRED CRAMER

" *Its scenery is not surpassed in variety, beauty, or grandeur by many districts in America. From the top of its mountains, the eye rests on landscapes lovely beyond description.* **"**

from The Captives of Abb's Valley:
A Legend of Frontier Life,
James Moore Brown

Mealtime for pileated woodpeckers   JOHN M. COFFMAN

A curious three-month-old raccoon   LYNDA RICHARDSON

Natural Bridge, purchased in 1774 from King George III by Thomas Jefferson for less than $5   KENT & DONNA DANNEN

Dog trainer communicating with his English pointer   LYNDA RICHARDSON

Walking up quail with a Brittany   LYNDA RICHARDSON

Pintails wheeling above Back Bay   LARRY R. DITTO

Banks of the Potomac River in Westmoreland State Park   CARR CLIFTON

" The passage of the Patowmac through the Blue ridge is perhaps one of the most stupendous scenes in nature.... "

Thomas Jefferson,
Writings

Spiderwort pushing through fallen leaves in Shenandoah National Park   WILLARD CLAY

Red fox   TIM CHRISTIE

Monarch butterfly on goldenrod   FRANK OBERLE / PHOTOGRAPHIC RESOURCES

Butterflyweed, important food plant for monarch butterflies   ROBERT E. LYONS

Peaks of Otter along the Blue Ridge Parkway   TOM ALGIRE

Wood duck   JOE MACHUDSPETH

Mabry Mill, home of the "best cornmeal in the country,"
along the Blue Ridge Parkway near Meadows of Dan   JEFF GNASS

Clouds cloaking a Blue Ridge mountaintop   D. L. WINSTON

Downy woodpecker hard at work on a February day   BILL LUBIC / PHOTOGRAPHIC RESOURCES

Milkweed   CUB KAHN

Sunrise over a piece of Virginia's past   JOHN M. COFFMAN

" *My native state is endeared to me by every tie which can attach the human heart.* "

Thomas Jefferson,
Report of Virginia Assembly, 1809

Sunrise over Shenandoah Valley, Page County   CUB KAHN

they made it possible

Virginia on my Mind would have been impossible to produce without the creative and technical skills of more than forty professional photographers. These men and women succeeded in a difficult task—capturing the many moods and faces of the Old Dominion.

From the mountains to the sea, Virginia contains a breathtaking array of beautiful images, but transforming these images onto film requires more than just a camera. It takes an eye for composition, technical expertise, long hours of work, and the sheer determination to obtain a memorable shot rather than a mere snapshot.

The photographers for *Virginia on my Mind* provided this extra skill and effort. They hiked, climbed, waited, and watched to get the best possible images from all parts of the state.

To all the excellent photographers who contributed to *Virginia on my Mind*, thank you.

Michael S. Sample,
Bill Schneider
Publishers, Falcon Press

Photographers in *Virginia on my Mind*

Gene Ahrens
Tom Algire
Fredrick D. Atwood
Erwin & Peggy Bauer
Alan D. Brier
Tim Christie
Willard Clay
Carr Clifton
John M. Coffman
Gary Cralle'
Fred Cramer
Steven Q. Croy
Kent & Donna Dannen
Derek Fell
William B. Folsom

James Frank
Jeff Gnass
P. A. Gormas
John M. Hall
Cub Kahn
Catherine Karnow
Zig Leszczynski
Jeff Lepore
Bill Lubic
Robert E. Lyons
Joe Mac Hudspeth
Pat & Bob Momich
David Muench
Frank Oberle
Robert Perron

Lynda Richardson
Mae Scanlan
Robert C. Simpson
Scott T. Smith
Steve Solum
John Lewis Stage
Connie Toops
Glenn Van Nimwegen
D. L. Winston
Tim Wright

And these photo agencies:
The Image Bank
Photographic Resources

acknowledgments

The publishers gratefully acknowledge the following sources:

Page 8 from *What Is It About Virginia?* by Guy Friddell. Copyright © 1966 by the author. Published by Dietz Press, Inc., Richmond, Virginia.

Pages 12, 44, and 88 from *Virginius Dabney's Virginia* by Virginius Dabney. Copyright © 1986 by the author. Published by Algonquin Books of Chapel Hill, North Carolina.

Page 16 from *This Quiet Dust* by William Styron. Copyright © 1982 by the author. Published by Random House, Inc., New York.

Page 20 from *Misty of Chincoteague* by Marguerite Henry. Copyright © 1947 by Rand McNally & Company.

Page 32 from *Bay Country* by Tom Horton. Copyright © 1987 by The Johns Hopkins University Press.

Pages 34, 70, and 74 from *Virginia Is a State of Mind* by Virginia Moore. Copyright © 1942 by E.P. Dutton & Co., Inc., New York.

Pages 42 and 90 from *Spencer's Mountain* by Earl Hamner, Jr. Copyright © 1961 by the author. Published by Dial Press, New York.

Page 46 from *Virginia Beautiful* by Wallace Nutting. Copyright © 1935 by the author. Published by Bonanza Books, a division of Crown Publishers, Inc., New York.

Page 48 from *Pilgrim at Tinker Creek* by Annie Dillard. Copyright © 1974 by the author. Published by Harper's Magazine Press in association with Harper & Row, New York.

Pages 52 and 98 from *The Virginia Way* by Guy Friddell. Copyright © 1973 by Burda GmbH. Published by Dr. Franz Burda, Offenburg, West Germany.

Page 54 from "The Last Parade" by Douglas Southall Freeman, as included in *Virginia Reader: A Treasury of Writings*, ed. by Francis Coleman Rosenberger. Copyright © 1948 by E.P. Dutton & Co., Inc., New York.

Pages 76 and 96 from *Virginia* by Michael Frome. Copyright © 1966 by the author. Published by Coward-McCann, New York.

Pages 78, 84, and 94 from *Vein of Iron* by Ellen Glasgow. Copyright © 1935 by the author, 1963 by First and Merchants National Bank of Richmond, Virginia.

Page 100 from *Up from Slavery: An Autobiography* by Booker T. Washington. Copyright © 1963 by Doubleday & Company, Inc., New York.

Page 104 from *The Captives of Abb's Valley: A Legend of Frontier Life* by James Moore Brown. Published in 1854 by the Presbyterian Board of Publisher, Philadelphia. Reprinted in 1978 by Garland Publishing, New York.

Page 108 from *Writings* by Thomas Jefferson, ed. by Merrill D. Peterson. Copyright © 1984 by Literary Classics of the United States.

about Guy Friddell

One of Virginia's best-known and most respected writers, Guy Friddell wrote the introduction to *Virginia on my Mind*. A resident of Virginia for more than fifty years, Friddell is a columnist for *The Virginian-Pilot* and the *Ledger-Star* in Norfolk. His work also appears in the *Richmond News Leader*. Friddell has written nine books, including six about Virginia. One of his books, *What is it about Virginia?*, received a commendation from the Virginia General Assembly, and his most recent book, *Hello, Hampton Roads,* received a first-place award from Virginia printers. Friddell and his wife live in Norfolk.

Doyle River Falls, Shenandoah National Park   WILLARD CLAY